Get to the heart of GCSE Biology with CGP!

There's a lot to learn for AQA's Grade 9-1 GCSE Biology exams... sometimes it can be hard to get motivated for a big revision session.

That's why we've made this fantastic little book — it's full of bite-sized tests, perfect for slotting into a convenient ten-minute slice of your life. And all the answers are included at the back, so it's easy to check your work. Very handy.

By the time you've reached the end, you'll have tested your knowledge of every GCSE Biology topic without even (well, hardly even) noticing...

CGP — still the best ☺

Our sole aim here at CGP is to produce the highest quality books — carefully written, immaculately presented and dangerously close to being funny.

Then we work our socks off to get them out to you — at the cheapest possible prices.

Published by CGP

Editors:
Charlotte Burrows, Daniel Fielding and Rachael Rogers.

ISBN: 978 1 78294 844 5

With thanks to Susan Alexander and Hayley Thompson for the proofreading.
With thanks to Emily Smith for the copyright research.

Clipart from Corel®
Illustrations by: Sandy Gardner Artist, email sandy@sandygardner.co.uk
Printed by W&G Baird Ltd, Antrim.

Based on the classic CGP style created by Richard Parsons.

Text, design, layout and original illustrations © Coordination Group Publications Ltd. (CGP) 2017
All rights reserved.

Photocopying this book is not permitted, even if you have a CLA licence.
Extra copies are available from CGP with next day delivery • 0800 1712 712 • www.cgpbooks.co.uk

Contents

Topics for Paper 1

Test 1: Cell Biology..2
Test 2: Cell Biology..4
Test 3: Organisation..6
Test 4: Organisation..8
Test 5: Organisation..10
Test 6: Infection and Response............................12
Test 7: Infection and Response............................14
Test 8: Infection and Response............................16
Test 9: Bioenergetics...18
Test 10: Bioenergetics...20

Mixed Tests for Paper 1

Test 11: Paper 1 Mixed Topics..............................22
Test 12: Paper 1 Mixed Topics..............................24
Test 13: Paper 1 Mixed Topics..............................26
Test 14: Paper 1 Mixed Topics..............................28
Test 15: Paper 1 Mixed Topics..............................30

Topics for Paper 2

Test 16: Homeostasis and Response....................32
Test 17: Homeostasis and Response....................34
Test 18: Homeostasis and Response....................36
Test 19: Inheritance, Variation and Evolution..........38
Test 20: Inheritance, Variation and Evolution..........40
Test 21: Inheritance, Variation and Evolution..........42
Test 22: Inheritance, Variation and Evolution..........44
Test 23: Ecology..46
Test 24: Ecology..48
Test 25: Ecology..50

Mixed Tests for Paper 2

Test 26: Paper 2 Mixed Topics..............................52
Test 27: Paper 2 Mixed Topics..............................54
Test 28: Paper 2 Mixed Topics..............................56
Test 29: Paper 2 Mixed Topics..............................58
Test 30: Paper 2 Mixed Topics..............................60

Answers...62

Progress Chart..67

Test 1: Cell Biology

There are **11 questions** in this test. Give yourself **10 minutes** to answer them all.

1. Why are cultures of microorganisms kept at 25 °C in school labs?

    A   It's too expensive to keep them at a higher temperature.

    B   Harmful pathogens are unlikely to grow at this temperature.

    C   Pathogens are killed at temperatures above 25 °C.

    [1]

2. Which of these parts are not found in a bacterial cell?

    A   Nucleus

    B   Cell membrane

    C   Cell wall

    [1]

3. Diffusion is where particles spread out from...

    A   ... an area of lower concentration to an area of higher concentration.

    B   ... an area of higher concentration to an area of lower concentration.

    [1]

4. Chloroplasts...

    A   ... strengthen a plant cell.

    B   ... store all the genetic material of a cell.

    C   ... absorb light energy to make glucose.

    [1]

5. True or False? "Specialised cells only exist in animals."

    A   True

    B   False

    [1]

6. If the concentration of water inside a cell is lower than outside the cell, what will the net movement of water molecules be?

    A   Into the cell

    B   Out of the cell

    [1]

7. When using a light microscope to view a slide, which lens should be selected to start with?

    A   Lowest-powered objective lens

    B   Highest-powered objective lens

    [1]

8. True or False? "Mitosis results in two cells that are genetically different."

    A   True

    B   False

    [1]

9. Give one way in which you could prevent a bacterial culture from becoming contaminated with unwanted microorganisms.

   ....
   [1]

10. What is a stem cell?

    ....

    ....

    ....
    [2]

11. Complete this diagram of an animal cell.

    mitochondrion

    nucleus

    ribosome

    Describe the roles of the following parts of a cell:

    Mitochondria ....

    ....

    Nucleus ....

    ....
    [4]

Test 2: Cell Biology

There are **12 questions** in this test. Give yourself **10 minutes** to answer them all.

1. When air is breathed in...
   - A ... oxygen is taken into the bloodstream and carbon dioxide is passed out.
   - B ... carbon dioxide is taken into the bloodstream and oxygen is passed out.

   [1]

2. True or False? "In human body cells, chromosomes usually come in pairs."
   - A True
   - B False

   [1]

3. True or False? "All plant cells lose the ability to differentiate at an early stage."
   - A True
   - B False

   [1]

4. What is the name for the process where perfume particles spread out in the air?
   - A Active transport
   - B Osmosis
   - C Diffusion

   [1]

5. What is a permanent vacuole?
   - A The space in a plant cell which is filled with cell sap.
   - B The space in a plant cell which contains chlorophyll.

   [1]

6. Which of these characteristics makes the alveoli efficient at gas exchange?
   - A They have thick walls.
   - B They have a large surface area.
   - C They don't have a good blood supply.

   [1]

7. Discs containing different antiseptic solutions are placed on an agar plate covered in bacteria. After several days, how could you compare the effectiveness of each antiseptic?
   - A Measure the inhibition zone around each disc.
   - B Measure the size of each disc.
   - C Observe the colour change around each disc.

   [1]

8. What happens inside a cell before mitosis takes place?
   - A The number of subcellular structures it has increases.
   - B One set of chromosomes is pulled to each end of the cell.
   - C The cell membrane divides.

   [1]

Topics for Paper 1: Cell Biology

9. Give one argument against using embryonic stem cells in medicine.

....

....
[1]

10. Electron microscopes have a higher resolution than light microscopes.
Give one reason why this is beneficial when viewing cells with an electron microscope.

....

....
[1]

11. Explain one way in which a nerve cell is adapted to carry out its specialised function.

....

....
[1]

12. Explain why root hairs in plants might use active transport.

....

....

....

....

....
[4]

15

Test 3: Organisation

There are **12 questions** in this test. Give yourself **10 minutes** to answer them all.

1. What is a tissue?

    A A collection of different types of cell that work together.

    B A collection of similar cells that work together.
    [1]

2. What colour is iodine solution in the presence of starch?

    A Blue-black

    B Browny-orange

    C Brick-red
    [1]

3. Where is bile produced and stored?

    A Bile is produced in the liver and stored in the gall bladder.

    B Bile is produced in the gall bladder and stored in the stomach.

    C Bile is produced in the stomach and stored in the pancreas.
    [1]

4. Which of these aren't features of arteries?

    A Elastic fibres

    B Thick walls

    C Valves
    [1]

5. Which type of tumour is cancerous?

    A Benign

    B Malignant
    [1]

6. Which of these is not a chamber of the heart?

    A Left ventricle

    B Right atrium

    C Vena cava
    [1]

7. True or False? "People who have problems with their immune system have an increased chance of suffering from communicable diseases."

    A True

    B False
    [1]

8. What's the function of palisade mesophyll tissue?

    A It covers the surface of a plant.

    B It's where photosynthesis happens.

    C It carries substances around a plant.
    [1]

Topics for Paper 1: Organisation

9. What is the role of protease enzymes?

   ....

   ....
   [1]

10. Describe the function of phloem tissue.

    ....

    ....
    [1]

11. Give two components of blood that are carried in the blood plasma.

    1. ....

    2. ....
    [2]

12. Describe what happens to an enzyme if the temperature is too high.

    ....

    ....

    ....

    ....
    [3]

Test 4: Organisation

There are **12 questions** in this test. Give yourself **10 minutes** to answer them all.

1. True or False? "Organ systems work together to form organs."
   - A True
   - B False

   [1]

2. What does phloem transport?
   - A Oxygen
   - B Sugars

   [1]

3. When breathing in, which structure(s) does air enter first?
   - A Alveoli
   - B Trachea
   - C Bronchi

   [1]

4. What is the function of white blood cells?
   - A They deliver nutrients around the body.
   - B They transport deoxygenated blood around the body.
   - C They defend the body against microorganisms.

   [1]

5. Why is the shape of an enzyme important for its function?
   - A So that it can squeeze through small gaps.
   - B So that it can enter the cells of the body.
   - C So that it fits the substance involved in the reaction it is catalysing.

   [1]

6. What is the name of the cells that control the opening and closing of stomata?
   - A Palisade cells
   - B Guard cells
   - C Meristem cells

   [1]

7. True or False? "Blood flows to the organs through veins."
   - A True
   - B False

   [1]

8. Which substance is broken down by amylase?
   - A Starch
   - B Glycerol
   - C Protein

   [1]

9. Give one advantage of using an artificial heart rather than transplanting a natural one.

   ....
   ....
   [1]

10. Give one risk factor that can increase a person's chance of developing liver disease.

    ....
    [1]

11. Describe what a benign tumour is.

    ....
    ....
    [1]

12. Explain how increasing air movement around a plant's leaves would affect the rate of transpiration.

    ....
    ....
    ....
    ....
    [4]

Test 5: Organisation

There are **12 questions** in this test. Give yourself **10 minutes** to answer them all.

1. The role of digestive enzymes is to...

    A ... catalyse the breakdown of food into smaller, soluble molecules.

    B ... catalyse the breakdown of food into smaller, insoluble molecules.
    [1]

2. Which of the following would you use to test for the presence of protein?

    A Biuret solution

    B Benedict's solution

    C Iodine solution
    [1]

3. Which of the following doesn't produce amylase?

    A The salivary glands

    B The pancreas

    C The stomach
    [1]

4. True or False? "Xylem tissue transports dissolved sugars around a plant."

    A True

    B False
    [1]

5. What artificial device can be used to keep arteries open and blood flowing?

    A A ventilator

    B A valve

    C A stent
    [1]

6. What substance, produced during photosynthesis, diffuses out of a plant via the stomata?

    A Glucose

    B Carbon dioxide

    C Oxygen
    [1]

7. Which word describes the loss of water from a plant's surface?

    A Translocation

    B Photosynthesis

    C Transpiration
    [1]

8. True or False? "Blood is a tissue."

    A True

    B False
    [1]

Topics for Paper 1: Organisation

9. The heart contains cells that act as a pacemaker.
   Where are these cells located in the heart?

   ....
   [1]

10. Other than disease, give two factors that can negatively effect a person's physical and mental health.

    1. ....

    2. ....
    [2]

11. Give two differences between arteries and veins.

    1. ....

    ....

    2. ....

    ....
    [2]

12. Explain how statins can reduce a person's risk of coronary heart disease.

    ....

    ....

    ....
    [2]

15

Topics for Paper 1: Organisation

Test 6: Infection and Response

There are **12 questions** in this test. Give yourself **10 minutes** to answer them all.

1. What is the first stage of testing a new medicinal drug?

   A The drug is tested on human cells and tissues in the lab.

   B The drug is tested on human volunteers in a clinical trial.

   [1]

2. How does the stomach help to defend the body against pathogens?

   A It secretes hydrochloric acid to kill pathogens.

   B It contains hairs to trap pathogens.

   C It secretes antibodies to kill pathogens.

   [1]

3. What's a microorganism that causes disease called?

   A An antibody

   B An antitoxin

   C A pathogen

   [1]

4. Which of the following is a chemical plant defence?

   A Waxy cuticle

   B Poison

   C Thorns

   [1]

5. Which drug was developed by Alexander Fleming?

   A Penicillin

   B Digitalis

   C Aspirin

   [1]

6. Gonorrhoea is a disease caused by...

   A ... protists.

   B ... viruses.

   C ... bacteria.

   [1]

7. True or False? "Antibiotics can kill viruses."

   A True

   B False

   [1]

8. Which type of drugs are used to control HIV?

   A Antibiotics

   B Antiretrovirals

   C Painkillers

   [1]

Topics for Paper 1: Infection and Response

9. Describe how the measles virus is spread.

   ....

   ....
   [1]

10. Explain why the tobacco mosaic virus (TMV) affects the growth of plants.

    ....

    ....

    ....
    [2]

11. Explain how mosquito nets help to prevent the spread of malaria.

    ....

    ....

    ....
    [2]

12. Explain how a lack of nitrate affects a plant's growth.

    ....

    ....

    ....
    [2]

Test 7: Infection and Response

There are **11 questions** in this test. Give yourself **10 minutes** to answer them all.

1. What is a placebo?

   A   A name given to the drug being tested in a clinical trial.

   B   A substance that looks like the drug being tested, but that doesn't do anything.

   C   A double dose of the drug being tested.

   [1]

2. Which disease in humans can be partly controlled by vaccinating poultry against the pathogen?

   A   Salmonella food poisoning

   B   Gonorrhoea

   C   Measles

   [1]

3. True or False? "Painkillers can reduce the symptoms of a disease and kill the pathogens."

   A   True

   B   False

   [1]

4. Which of the following diseases are young children often vaccinated against?

   A   HIV

   B   Salmonella food poisoning

   C   Measles

   [1]

5. True or False? "Preclinical trials help to find the optimum dose for a drug."

   A   True

   B   False

   [1]

6. Why are monoclonal antibodies not used as widely as was originally hoped?

   A   They can't be used to detect disease.

   B   They cause side effects.

   C   They don't treat diseases.

   [1]

7. Phagocytosis is the process in which white blood cells...

   A   ...release antibodies.

   B   ...release antitoxins.

   C   ...engulf and digest foreign cells.

   [1]

8. Which type of pathogen causes rose black spot on leaves?

   A   A fungus

   B   A bacterium

   C   A virus

   [1]

Topics for Paper 1: Infection and Response

9. How do viruses make you feel ill?

   ....

   ....

   ....
   [2]

10. How does the nose help to defend the body against disease?

    ....

    ....
    [2]

11. Explain how vaccination can protect against a disease.

    ....

    ....

    ....

    ....
    [3]

Topics for Paper 1: Infection and Response

Test 8: Infection and Response

There are **11 questions** in this test. Give yourself **10 minutes** to answer them all.

1. What is penicillin?
   - A   An antibiotic
   - B   An anti-viral drug
   - C   A painkiller

   [1]

2. True or False? "For a large outbreak of an infectious disease to be prevented, everyone must be vaccinated against it."
   - A   True
   - B   False

   [1]

3. What do white blood cells produce to help defend against pathogens?
   - A   Antigens
   - B   Antibiotics
   - C   Antibodies

   [1]

4. Which of the following diseases is not spread by sexual contact?
   - A   HIV
   - B   Gonorrhoea
   - C   Measles

   [1]

5. Mimicry is an example of which type of plant defence?
   - A   Mechanical
   - B   Chemical
   - C   Physical

   [1]

6. Which of the following diseases is caused by a protist?
   - A   Measles
   - B   Malaria
   - C   HIV

   [1]

7. Which of these statements about bacteria is false?
   - A   Bacteria damage cells by living and replicating inside them.
   - B   Some bacteria reproduce really quickly in the body.
   - C   Bacteria can produce toxins.

   [1]

8. Aspirin was developed from a chemical found in...
   - A   ...foxgloves.
   - B   ...mould.
   - C   ...willow.

   [1]

Topics for Paper 1: Infection and Response

9. Give one way in which rose black spot disease can be treated.

   ....
   [1]

10. What is a double-blind trial and why is it used in clinical trials?

    ....
    ....
    ....
    ....
    ....
    [3]

11. Describe how monoclonal antibodies can be used to treat cancer.

    ....
    ....
    ....
    ....
    ....
    [3]

Test 9: Bioenergetics

There are **12 questions** in this test. Give yourself **10 minutes** to answer them all.

1. During exercise, which of the following happens?

   A Just your breathing rate increases.

   B Just your breath volume increases.

   C Your breathing rate and your breath volume increases.

   [1]

2. Which of these is not a limiting factor of photosynthesis?

   A Light

   B Temperature

   C Oxygen

   [1]

3. True or False? "Aerobic respiration occurs in plants and animals all the time."

   A True

   B False

   [1]

4. True or False? "The starch in plants that's created from glucose is insoluble."

   A True

   B False

   [1]

5. Which type of respiration transfers more energy?

   A Aerobic respiration

   B Anaerobic respiration

   [1]

6. Respiration is an...

   A ... exothermic reaction.

   B ... endothermic reaction.

   [1]

7. Aerobic respiration produces...

   A ... glucose.

   B ... carbon dioxide only.

   C ... water and carbon dioxide.

   [1]

8. What would you expect to happen to the volume of oxygen produced by pondweed if light intensity increased, and it was the limiting factor?

   A It would increase.

   B It would stay the same.

   C It would decrease.

   [1]

Topics for Paper 1: Bioenergetics

9. Why do muscles start respiring anaerobically during vigorous exercise?

....

....
[1]

10. Name the supporting material that plants make using glucose.

....

Which part of the cell is made using this material?

....
[2]

11. Complete the equation for photosynthesis.

.... + water ⟶ .... + oxygen
[2]

12. Describe how the body gets rid of the lactic acid that builds up in the muscles.

....

....

....
[2]

15

Test 10: Bioenergetics

There are **12 questions** in this test. Give yourself **10 minutes** to answer them all.

1. True or False? "Anaerobic respiration requires oxygen."

   A True

   B False

   [1]

2. Rania walked to catch the bus, but Mia was late so had to run. Whose heart rate will be higher?

   A Rania

   B Mia

   [1]

3. Which of these things are not used by plants to make proteins?

   A Glucose

   B Nitrate ions

   C Lipids

   [1]

4. Other than oxygen, what does photosynthesis produce?

   A Carbon dioxide

   B Water

   C Glucose

   [1]

5. True or False? "As the level of carbon dioxide increases, the rate of photosynthesis will always increase."

   A True

   B False

   [1]

6. Which chemical symbol represents a product of aerobic respiration?

   A $C_6H_{12}O_6$

   B O_2

   C CO_2

   [1]

7. Which of the following is produced when yeast cells respire anaerobically?

   A Glucose

   B Ethanol

   C Lactic acid

   [1]

8. What is a single lipid molecule made up of?

   A One molecule of glycerol and three fatty acids.

   B One fatty acid and three molecules of glycerol.

   C Three molecules of glycerol and three fatty acids.

   [1]

Topics for Paper 1: Bioenergetics

9. What is meant by the term 'metabolism'?

   ....

   ....
   [1]

10. Explain what happens to the rate of photosynthesis if a plant is put in a dark place.

    ....

    ....

    ....
    [2]

11. Describe what is meant by muscle fatigue and state when it occurs.

    ....

    ....

    ....
    [2]

12. Give two uses of the energy released by respiration.

    1. ....

    ....

    2. ....

    ....
    [2]

Test 11: Paper 1 Mixed Topics

There are **11 questions** in this test. Give yourself **10 minutes** to answer them all.

1. Phloem is made up of...

   A ... hollow tubes of dead cells strengthened by lignin.

   B ... lots of small holes called stomata, to allow gas exchange.

   C ... columns of elongated cells with small pores in the end walls.

   [1]

2. Why is a new drug tested on live animals?

   A Because it's cheaper than testing on humans.

   B To test how well the drug works compared to a placebo.

   C To make sure it's safe before testing on humans.

   [1]

3. Stem cells from adult bone marrow can turn into...

   A ...any type of cell.

   B ...many types of cell.

   C ...blood cells only.

   [1]

4. Which type of microscope has a higher magnification?

   A Electron microscope

   B Light microscope

   [1]

5. True or False? "Increasing the temperature always causes the rate of photosynthesis to increase."

   A True

   B False

   [1]

6. True or False? "Severe physical illness can lead to the development of mental illness."

   A True

   B False

   [1]

7. Which of the following is a physical plant defence?

   A Poisons

   B Mimicry

   C Cellulose cell walls

   [1]

8. Chromosomes are...

   A ... a type of organelle where photosynthesis occurs.

   B ... really long molecules of DNA, which contain genes.

   C ... a type of cell involved in reproduction.

   [1]

9. Give two ways that an exchange surface in animals may be specialised for its function.

1. ....

2. ....
[2]

10. How do plants make proteins?

....

....

....

....
[2]

11. Malignant tumours are more dangerous than benign tumours.
Explain why.

....

....

....

....

....
[3]

Test 12: Paper 1 Mixed Topics

There are **11 questions** in this test. Give yourself **10 minutes** to answer them all.

1. Which part of the blood is responsible for blood clotting?

   A   Red blood cells

   B   White blood cells

   C   Platelets

   [1]

2. True or False? "Vaccinations involve injecting small amounts of dead or inactive pathogens into the body."

   A   True

   B   False

   [1]

3. What are monoclonal antibodies produced from?

   A   Clones of a single cell.

   B   Clones of different cells.

   [1]

4. How are root cells specialised for absorbing water and nutrients?

   A   They are round.

   B   They have bacteria on their surface.

   C   The cells are shaped like long hairs.

   [1]

5. True or False? "Some types of cancer can be triggered by a viral infection."

   A   True

   B   False

   [1]

6. What is a cell called when it has differentiated?

   A   An unspecialised cell.

   B   A specialised cell.

   C   A stem cell.

   [1]

7. What is an advantage of using monoclonal antibodies to treat cancer?

   A   There are no side effects.

   B   They bind to lots of different cells in the body to make sure they aren't cancerous.

   C   They can be used to kill cancer cells without harming other cells in the body.

   [1]

8. When culturing microorganisms, why should you sterilise the Petri dishes you'll be using?

   A   To stop drops of condensation falling onto the agar.

   B   To prevent contamination by unwanted microorganisms.

   C   To allow inhibition zones to form.

   [1]

9. Name one non-specific defence system of the human body against pathogens.

....
[1]

10. Explain why lactic acid can build up during vigorous exercise.

....

....

....

....
[3]

11. Describe what happens in the heart of someone with coronary heart disease.

....

....

....

....
[3]

Test 13: Paper 1 Mixed Topics

There are **12 questions** in this test. Give yourself **10 minutes** to answer them all.

1. What is the function of cellulose?

   A To strengthen the cell walls in plants

   B To make proteins

   C To help with respiration

   [1]

2. True or False? "The DNA in plant cells is found within a nucleus."

   A True

   B False

   [1]

3. The leaf is an example of a plant...

   A ... tissue.

   B ... organ.

   C ... organ system.

   [1]

4. What happens to enzymes at high temperatures?

   A They divide, producing more enzymes.

   B They start to attack the cells in the body.

   C They denature.

   [1]

5. True or False? "An organ is a group of similar cells that work together to carry out a particular function."

   A True

   B False

   [1]

6. The right ventricle pumps blood to...

   A ... the lungs.

   B ... the brain.

   C ... the muscles.

   [1]

7. Which of the following plant tissues can differentiate into lots of different types of cell?

   A Epidermal tissue

   B Mesophyll tissue

   C Meristem tissue

   [1]

8. Oxygen debt is the amount of extra oxygen...

   A ... taken in during exercise because the breathing rate increases.

   B ... needed to react with the build up of lactic acid and remove it from cells.

   [1]

9. Explain what is meant by the term 'cell differentiation'.

   ....

   ....
   [1]

10. Name a bacterial disease and give one symptom of this disease.

    ....

    ....
    [2]

11. What is the function of xylem vessels?

    ....

    Give one way in which they're adapted for this function.

    ....

    ....
    [2]

12. What is osmosis?

    ....

    ....

    ....
    [2]

Test 14: Paper 1 Mixed Topics

There are **12 questions** in this test. Give yourself **10 minutes** to answer them all.

1. Palisade mesophyll cells are adapted for photosynthesis. Which of these characteristics would help them to carry out this specialised function?

   A   Having a thick cell wall.

   B   Containing lots of chloroplasts.

   C   Being situated at the bottom of a leaf.
   [1]

2. What happens at the end of mitosis?

   A   The cell grows and increases its number of sub-cellular structures.

   B   The cytoplasm and cell membrane divide to form two identical cells.

   C   DNA is replicated to form two copies of each chromosome.
   [1]

3. Where in a cell do most of the reactions involved in aerobic respiration take place?

   A   The cytoplasm

   B   The nucleus

   C   The mitochondria
   [1]

4. True or False? "Some drugs have been made from chemicals originally found in plants."

   A   True

   B   False
   [1]

5. Some of the glucose from photosynthesis is used for...

   A   ... transpiration.

   B   ... respiration.
   [1]

6. If you place a slice of potato in a solution that has a higher sugar concentration than the fluid inside the potato, the potato will...

   A   ... release water and decrease in mass.

   B   ... absorb water and increase in mass.
   [1]

7. The 'lock and key' model is used to describe...

   A   ... the way cells divide in mitosis.

   B   ... the rate of diffusion.

   C   ... the action of enzymes.
   [1]

8. True or False? "Respiration provides the energy needed for cell metabolism."

   A   True

   B   False
   [1]

9. What happens when a heart valve becomes leaky?

   ....

   ....
   [1]

10. Explain how having a large surface area affects the rate of diffusion across an exchange surface.

    ....

    ....

    ....
    [2]

11. Name the blood vessel that carries blood from the lungs to the heart.

    ....

    Name the blood vessel that carries blood from the heart to the organs.

    ....
    [2]

12. What is a hybridoma cell made from?

    ....

    ....
    [2]

Test 15: Paper 1 Mixed Topics

There are **12 questions** in this test. Give yourself **10 minutes** to answer them all.

1. Which process allows glucose to move from a higher concentration in the gut to a lower concentration in the blood?

   A Active transport

   B Osmosis

   C Diffusion

   [1]

2. True or False? "The inheritance of faulty genes is the only risk factor for cancer."

   A True

   B False

   [1]

3. The human heart pumps blood around the body in a...

   A ... single circulatory system.

   B ... double circulatory system.

   C ... triple circulatory system.

   [1]

4. True or False? "Active transport means that cells can absorb minerals against the concentration gradient."

   A True

   B False

   [1]

5. What is the correct equation for anaerobic respiration in muscles?

   A glucose + oxygen → carbon dioxide + water

   B glucose → lactic acid

   C glucose → ethanol + carbon dioxide

   [1]

6. It is possible to detect a plant with nitrate deficiency because it will...

   A ... show stunted growth.

   B ... have patches of decay.

   C ... have abnormal growths.

   [1]

7. True or False? "Stems, roots and leaves are all plant organs."

   A True

   B False

   [1]

8. Health is...

   A ... the state of physical well-being only.

   B ... the state of mental and emotional well-being only.

   C ... the state of physical and mental well-being.

   [1]

Mixed Tests for Paper 1

9. Complete this equation for magnification.

$$\text{magnification} = \frac{\dots\dots\dots\dots\dots\dots\dots\dots\dots\dots}{\dots\dots\dots\dots\dots\dots\dots\dots\dots\dots}$$

[1]

10. Give two examples of diseases that can be caused directly by smoking.

    1. ....

    2. ....
    [2]

11. A student investigates the effect of pH on the reaction rate of amylase on starch solution. Give one example of a variable that must be controlled in this investigation.

    ....

    How could this variable be controlled?

    ....
    [2]

12. A bacterial cell undergoes binary fission every 20 minutes.
    If there was a single cell to begin with, how many cells will there be after 2 hours?

    ....

    ....

    ....
    [2]

Test 16: Homeostasis and Response

There are **11 questions** in this test. Give yourself **10 minutes** to answer them all.

1. In a plant root, does auxin increase or inhibit growth?

   A   Increase

   B   Inhibit

   [1]

2. True or False? "Excess ions are removed from the body via the kidneys."

   A   True

   B   False

   [1]

3. Which of the following substances are reabsorbed by the kidneys?

   A   Glucose, water and ions.

   B   Glucose, water and urea.

   C   ADH, glucose and ions.

   [1]

4. Which is the correct pathway for stimuli along a reflex arc?

   A   relay neurone → sensory neurone → motor neurone

   B   sensory neurone → motor neurone → relay neurone

   C   sensory neurone → relay neurone → motor neurone

   [1]

5. The cerebellum is responsible for...

   A   ... consciousness and intelligence.

   B   ... muscle coordination.

   C   ... controlling unconscious activities.

   [1]

6. The gland which releases thyroxine is...

   A   ... the pituitary gland.

   B   ... the adrenal gland.

   C   ... the thyroid gland.

   [1]

7. Why do muscles 'shiver'?

   A   To store energy to warm the body.

   B   To create friction within the body.

   C   To release energy to warm the body.

   [1]

8. In dialysis, urea passes from...

   A   ... the blood into the dialysis fluid.

   B   ... the dialysis fluid into the blood.

   [1]

9. List three internal conditions that your body needs to keep constant to survive.

   1. ....

   2. ....

   3. ....
   [3]

10. Explain what Type 1 diabetes is, and why it is dangerous.

    ....

    ....

    ....
    [2]

11. Briefly explain what long-sightedness is.

    ....

    ....

    ....

    ....
    [2]

Test 17: Homeostasis and Response

There are **11 questions** in this test. Give yourself **10 minutes** to answer them all.

1. What is the hormone that controls the 'fight or flight' response?
   A Thyroxine
   B Adrenaline
   C Glucagon
   [1]

2. True or False? "Caffeine can affect a person's reaction time."
   A True
   B False
   [1]

3. Within the eye, the lens is responsible for...
   A ... controlling the diameter of the pupil.
   B ... carrying impulses to the brain.
   C ... focusing light onto the retina.
   [1]

4. A sprouting seed is planted so that the shoot is pointing sideways. Which side will grow faster?
   A The lower side
   B The upper side
   [1]

5. True or False? "With modern day medicine, the treatment of brain disorders is easy."
   A True
   B False
   [1]

6. Reaction time is the time it takes for someone to...
   A ... detect a stimulus.
   B ... respond to a stimulus.
   C ... remember something.
   [1]

7. What is secreted by the pancreas when blood glucose levels fall?
   A Glucose
   B Insulin
   C Glucagon
   [1]

8. True or False? "Hormones have longer-lasting effects than nervous impulses."
   A True
   B False
   [1]

Topics for Paper 2: Homeostasis and Response

9. What is the role of LH in the menstrual cycle?

   ....
   [1]

10. What is meant by the term homeostasis?

    ....

    ....

    ....

    ....
    [3]

11. Explain how blood vessels help to reduce core body temperature when it gets too high.

    ....

    ....

    ....

    ....
    [3]

Test 18: Homeostasis and Response

There are **11 questions** in this test. Give yourself **10 minutes** to answer them all.

1. Which of the following is a barrier method of contraception?

   A   Diaphragm

   B   Contraceptive patch

   C   Intrauterine device

   [1]

2. On which side of a plant shoot will more auxin accumulate when the shoot is exposed to light?

   A   The side in the light.

   B   The shaded side.

   C   Equally on the light and shaded sides.

   [1]

3. What is the central nervous system made up of?

   A   The brain and receptors

   B   The brain and the spinal cord

   C   The spinal cord and receptors

   [1]

4. True or False? "To look at near objects, the ciliary muscles must contract."

   A   True

   B   False

   [1]

5. How can ethene be used commercially?

   A   To stimulate the growth of plant stems

   B   To grow plant cells in tissue culture

   C   To speed up the fruit ripening process

   [1]

6. How do capillaries change when body temperature gets too low?

   A   They constrict

   B   They dilate

   [1]

7. True or False? "The blood sugar level of someone with Type 1 diabetes is always dangerously low."

   A   True

   B   False

   [1]

8. How many days does the menstrual cycle usually last for?

   A   52 days

   B   7 days

   C   28 days

   [1]

Topics for Paper 2: Homeostasis and Response

9. Describe one possible treatment option for people whose kidneys are not functioning properly.

   ....

   ....
   [1]

10. If you set up an experiment where you have plant A directly under a lamp and plant B to one side of a lamp, what difference would there be between the plants after a few days?

    ....

    ....

    Briefly explain what causes this difference.

    ....

    ....

    ....
    [3]

11. What type of neurone transmits impulses to an effector in the nervous system?

    ....

    Give an example of an effector, and describe how it responds to a stimulus.

    ....

    ....
    [3]

15

Topics for Paper 2: Homeostasis and Response

Test 19: Inheritance, Variation and Evolution

There are **11 questions** in this test. Give yourself **10 minutes** to answer them all.

1. True or False? "It's completely random which organisms survive and pass on their genes to the next generation."

   A   True
   B   False
   [1]

2. Gregor Mendel was an Austrian monk who...

   A   ... discovered that men have a Y chromosome.
   B   ... showed that embryonic stem cells can differentiate into any type of cell.
   C   .... investigated how pea plants pass on their characteristics from one generation to the next.
   [1]

3. How many chromosomes does a human gamete have?

   A   46
   B   12
   C   23
   [1]

4. True or False? "Fossils can be formed from an organism's footprints and burrows that have been preserved over time."

   A   True
   B   False
   [1]

5. How are genes 'cut out' from chromosomes in genetic engineering?

   A   Using enzymes
   B   Using bacteria
   C   Using a knife
   [1]

6. What sex chromosomes does someone who is biologically male have?

   A   XY
   B   XXX
   C   XX
   [1]

7. Why does adult cell cloning require an electric shock?

   A   To add DNA to the cell.
   B   To give the cell energy to move.
   C   To help the cell start to divide.
   [1]

8. True or False? "A mutation always has an effect on a species."

   A   True
   B   False
   [1]

Topics for Paper 2: Inheritance, Variation and Evolution

9. Give two pieces of evidence that support Darwin's theory of evolution.

   1. ....

   ....

   2. ....

   ....
   [2]

10. Suggest two reasons why someone may be against embryonic screening.

    1. ....

    ....

    2. ....

    ....
    [2]

11. Explain why a species that reproduces asexually may be at a higher risk from a change in the environment than a species that reproduces sexually.

    ....

    ....

    ....

    ....
    [3]

Test 20: Inheritance, Variation and Evolution

There are **12 questions** in this test. Give yourself **10 minutes** to answer them all.

1. True or False? "The alleles for cystic fibrosis and polydactyly are both dominant."

    A   True

    B   False

    [1]

2. If a farmer wants to increase the meat yield of his cows, he would breed together...

    A   ... the biggest cows.

    B   ... those that produced the most milk.

    C   ... those with a gentle temperament.

    [1]

3. What structure does DNA have?

    A   A long, single, straight chain

    B   A triple helix structure

    C   A double helix structure

    [1]

4. How often do mutations result in a new phenotype?

    A   Always

    B   Often

    C   Very rarely

    [1]

5. What do evolutionary trees show?

    A   Evolutionary relationships

    B   Parental relationships

    C   Genetic disorders

    [1]

6. What is a problem that could result from patients not finishing a course of antibiotics?

    A   Antibiotic resistance increases in bacteria.

    B   Antibiotic resistance increases in viruses.

    C   Immunity to disease increases in humans.

    [1]

7. How many cell divisions occur during meiosis?

    A   1

    B   2

    C   4

    [1]

8. What is the correct order of classification groups?

    A   Kingdom → Genus → Class → Order → Family → Phylum → Species

    B   Family → Phylum → Species → Order → Kingdom → Genus → Class

    C   Kingdom → Phylum → Class → Order → Family → Genus → Species

    [1]

Topics for Paper 2: Inheritance, Variation and Evolution

© CGP — not to be photocopied

9. What is a fossil?

....

....
[1]

10. What is meant by embryo screening?

....

....
[1]

11. Describe the idea that Mendel proposed as a result of his research on pea plants.

....

....

....

....
[2]

12. Explain why speciation might occur if two populations of the same species are isolated from one another by a flood.

....

....

....

....

....
[3]

Test 21: Inheritance, Variation and Evolution

There are **11 questions** in this test. Give yourself **10 minutes** to answer them all.

1. What effect do mutations have on variation?

   A They decrease it.

   B They increase it.

   C There is no effect.

   [1]

2. If a dog with long hair (Hh) was bred with a dog with short hair (hh), what possible combinations of alleles could be produced?

   A hh

   B HH

   C Hh, hh

   [1]

3. True or False? "The fossil record provides evidence for evolution."

   A True

   B False

   [1]

4. True or False? "Cloning can reduce the gene pool."

   A True

   B False

   [1]

5. True or False? "Many fungi can reproduce asexually or sexually."

   A True

   B False

   [1]

6. What is an organism's genotype?

   A The characteristics that the organism has.

   B The alleles that the organism has.

   [1]

7. When human gametes join at fertilisation, what numbers of chromosomes are combined?

   A 46 + 46 = 92

   B 23 + 23 = 46

   C 46 + 23 = 69

   [1]

8. What is the main idea behind Darwin's theory of evolution by natural selection?

   A There is variation in a population. Those more suited to the environment will be more likely to survive and pass on their characteristics.

   B Individuals develop characteristics during their lifetimes, which make them more suited to their environment. They pass these onto their offspring.

   [1]

Topics for Paper 2: Inheritance, Variation and Evolution

9. Give two factors that might cause a species to become extinct.

1. ....

....

2. ....

....
[2]

10. The diagram shows a simple evolutionary tree.
Use it to describe how the whale and shark are related,
in terms of distant and recent ancestors.

....

....

....

....
[2]

11. Explain how sexual reproduction produces variation.

....

....

....

....

....
[3]

Test 22: Inheritance, Variation and Evolution

There are **11 questions** in this test. Give yourself **10 minutes** to answer them all.

1. When an individual has one dominant and one recessive allele...

   A ... the recessive allele is expressed.

   B ... both alleles are expressed.

   C ... the dominant allele is expressed.

   [1]

2. If an individual has only one copy of the cystic fibrosis allele then they...

   A ... have cystic fibrosis.

   B ... are a carrier of cystic fibrosis.

   [1]

3. Which scientist was well known for his work on the theory of speciation?

   A Carl Woese

   B Carl Linnaeus

   C Alfred Wallace

   [1]

4. True or False? "Some people think embryo screening is ethically wrong."

   A True

   B False

   [1]

5. What is one advantage of asexual reproduction?

   A There's variation in the offspring.

   B The offspring are more likely to survive a change in the environment.

   C It requires only one parent.

   [1]

6. True or False? "A population that has undergone speciation will eventually be able to breed together again."

   A True

   B False

   [1]

7. During pregnancy, what chance is there of a woman having a baby boy?

   A 50%

   B 25%

   C 75%

   [1]

8. True or False? "Selective breeding can happen without human intervention."

   A True

   B False

   [1]

Topics for Paper 2: Inheritance, Variation and Evolution

9. What is the role of a vector in genetic engineering?

   ....

   ....

   Give one example of a vector used in genetic engineering.

   ....
   [2]

10. A tall pea plant with two dominant 'T' alleles and a dwarf pea plant with two recessive 't' alleles are crossed to produce a pea plant with the genotype Tt. What will the new plant's phenotype be? Explain your answer.

    ....

    ....

    ....

    ....
    [2]

11. What does a single nucleotide consist of?

    ....

    ....

    ....
    [3]

Topics for Paper 2: Inheritance, Variation and Evolution

Test 23: Ecology

There are **12 questions** in this test. Give yourself **10 minutes** to answer them all.

1. Which is the best definition of an extremophile?

   A An organism that is able to live in only one type of environment.

   B An organism that is adapted to living in very extreme conditions.

   C An organism that is adapted to living in safe conditions.

   [1]

2. Why is fishing net size important in the conservation of fish stocks?

   A It saves money.

   B It saves space on the fishing boats.

   C It stops the collection of 'unwanted' fish.

   [1]

3. What type of compost should people choose to avoid contributing to global warming?

   A Peat-free compost

   B Compost made using peat

   [1]

4. Mycoprotein is used to make...

   A ... protein-rich food that's suitable for vegetarians.

   B ... a food that contains no protein but is suitable for vegetarians.

   [1]

5. Which of the following factors do plants compete for?

   A Light, space, water and mates

   B Water, mates, space and mineral ions

   C Space, water, mineral ions and light

   [1]

6. True or False? "Global warming could reduce the Earth's biodiversity."

   A True

   B False

   [1]

7. What does a change in the distribution of an animal mean?

   A A change in its numbers.

   B A change in where it lives.

   C A change in the food it eats.

   [1]

8. True or False? "A pyramid of biomass shows the number of organisms at each stage of a food chain."

   A True

   B False

   [1]

9. How does the amount of biomass change along a food chain?

   ....

   ....
   [1]

10. How does respiration contribute to the carbon cycle?

    ....
    [1]

11. Give two types of programme that people have set up to protect ecosystems and biodiversity.

    1. ....

    ....

    2. ....

    ....
    [2]

12. Suggest three biotic factors that might cause a decrease in the population of a species.

    1. ....

    2. ....

    3. ....
    [3]

Test 24: Ecology

There are **11 questions** in this test. Give yourself **10 minutes** to answer them all.

1. How can you study the distribution of organisms in a way that will give reproducible results?

   A Always take the sample from the same place.

   B Use a small sample size.

   C Use a large sample size.

   [1]

2. What is global warming?

   A An increase in the level of oxygen within the Earth's atmosphere.

   B A decrease in the level of carbon dioxide within the Earth's atmosphere.

   C An increase in the average global temperature.

   [1]

3. Which of the following is an abiotic factor?

   A Temperature

   B New predators arriving

   C New pathogens arriving

   [1]

4. How can you investigate the effect of temperature on the rate of decay of fresh milk?

   A By measuring the pH change of the milk.

   B By measuring the temperature change of the milk.

   [1]

5. What is the definition of an apex predator?

   A A carnivore that only eats herbivores.

   B A carnivore with no predators.

   C A carnivore with predators.

   [1]

6. A producer...

   A ... is eaten by secondary consumers.

   B ... makes glucose from photosynthesis.

   C ... is also a primary consumer.

   [1]

7. True or False? "Sewage produced by humans can pollute lakes, rivers and oceans."

   A True

   B False

   [1]

8. If a new predator arrives in an area, will the size of the prey population increase or decrease?

   A Increase

   B Decrease

   [1]

Topics for Paper 2: Ecology

9. Give two biological factors that are a threat to food security.

   1. ....

   2. ....
   [2]

10. Give two reasons why large-scale deforestation has occurred in tropical areas.

    1. ....

    2. ....
    [2]

11. Why is it important to maintain fish stocks at a level where fish continue to breed?

    ....

    ....

    Briefly explain how fishing quotas play a role in maintaining fish stocks.

    ....

    ....

    ....
    [3]

Test 25: Ecology

There are **12 questions** in this test. Give yourself **10 minutes** to answer them all.

1. True or False? "To study the effect of an abiotic factor on the distribution of an organism, you could use a transect."

   A   True
   B   False
   [1]

2. A species being outcompeted by another species is an example of...

   A   ... a biotic factor.
   B   ... an abiotic factor.
   [1]

3. Which of these would be represented by the smallest bar on a pyramid of biomass?

   A   Grass
   B   Rabbit
   C   Fox
   [1]

4. *Fusarium* is grown using...

   A   ... glucose syrup.
   B   ... protein.
   C   ... methane.
   [1]

5. True or False? "None of the Sun's energy is lost throughout a food chain."

   A   True
   B   False
   [1]

6. It's important to maintain a high level of biodiversity because...

   A   ... it helps ecosystems to be more stable.
   B   ... it will decrease the amount of waste.
   C   ... it will increase global warming.
   [1]

7. Which of the following is not a method of increasing the efficiency of food production?

   A   Allowing livestock to roam freely.
   B   Feeding livestock high protein foods.
   C   Restricting movement of livestock.
   [1]

8. True or False? "In the water cycle, water falls from clouds in a process called evaporation."

   A   True
   B   False
   [1]

Topics for Paper 2: Ecology

9. What is interdependence?

   ....

   ....
   [1]

10. State two environmental changes that could affect the distribution of species.

    1. ....

    2. ....
    [2]

11. Explain how draining peat bogs to produce compost contributes to global warming.

    ....

    ....

    ....

    ....
    [2]

12. Give two advantages of using GM crops.

    1. ....

    ....

    2. ....

    ....
    [2]

15

Test 26: Paper 2 Mixed Topics

There are **12 questions** in this test. Give yourself **10 minutes** to answer them all.

1. Which of these is a problem caused by the rapid rise in the world's population?

   A   Less carbon dioxide in the atmosphere

   B   More waste is being produced

   C   More diversity amongst people

   [1]

2. True or False? "Surgical sterilisation in males involves cutting the sperm duct and so is a permanent method of contraception."

   A   True

   B   False

   [1]

3. Deforestation is...

   A   ... growing crops in forests.

   B   ... renaming forests.

   C   ... cutting down trees.

   [1]

4. What combination of hormones can be given to a woman to improve her fertility?

   A   Oestrogen and progesterone

   B   FSH and LH

   C   Oestrogen and LH

   [1]

5. True or False? "The pituitary gland secretes hormones that act on other glands to trigger the release of other hormones."

   A   True

   B   False

   [1]

6. What is the correct base pairing in a DNA molecule?

   A   A and T, C and G

   B   G and T, C and A

   C   A and G, T and C

   [1]

7. Which of these statements best describes Lamarck's theory of evolution?

   A   Changes in an organism's characteristics during their lifetime can be inherited by their offspring.

   B   Only organisms with characteristics suitable for their environment will survive.

   [1]

8. True or False? "Some gametes are genetically identical to each other."

   A   True

   B   False

   [1]

9. Why is it important for your body temperature to be maintained at a certain level?

   ....

   ....
   [1]

10. What is an MRI scan of the brain used to show?

    ....

    ....
    [1]

11. Describe the process of tissue culture.

    ....

    ....

    ....
    [2]

12. What is inbreeding?

    ....

    ....

    Explain one problem associated with inbreeding.

    ....

    ....

    ....
    [3]

15

Test 27: Paper 2 Mixed Topics

There are **12 questions** in this test. Give yourself **10 minutes** to answer them all.

1. How many bases are needed to code for one amino acid?

   A   1
   B   3
   C   6
   [1]

2. True or False? "An organism's characteristics can only be determined by the genes it has inherited."

   A   True
   B   False
   [1]

3. Which of the following may be used to control Type 2 diabetes?

   A   Taking injections of glucagon.
   B   Avoiding all forms of exercise.
   C   Eating a carbohydrate-controlled diet.
   [1]

4. What is *Fusarium*?

   A   A fungus
   B   A bacterium
   C   A plant
   [1]

5. True or False? "Embryo transplants can be used to clone plants."

   A   True
   B   False
   [1]

6. Alfred Russel Wallace came up with the idea of...

   A   ... classifying living things into groups.
   B   ... the inheritance of 'hereditary units'.
   C   ... evolution by natural selection.
   [1]

7. What is meant when a reflex arc is described as 'automatic'?

   A   It only involves the brain.
   B   It only involves the conscious part of the brain.
   C   It doesn't involve the conscious part of the brain.
   [1]

8. An ecosystem is the interaction...

   A   ... between the individuals of a species that live in a habitat.
   B   ... between the community of living organisms.
   C   ... between the community of living organisms and the non-living parts of their environment.
   [1]

9. Which gas is biogas mainly made up of?

    ....
    [1]

10. Complete this diagram of an eye.

    ....

    ....
    [2]

11. Give two examples of a hormonal contraceptive.

    1. ....

    2. ....
    [2]

12. Explain why new, antibiotic-resistant strains of bacteria can quickly spread.

    ....

    ....

    ....
    [2]

Test 28: Paper 2 Mixed Topics

There are **12 questions** in this test. Give yourself **10 minutes** to answer them all.

1. What four bases does DNA contain?
   A   A, B, C and D
   B   A, C, G and T
   C   A, C, E and G
   [1]

2. The level of glucose in the blood is monitored by the...
   A   ... pancreas.
   B   ... thyroid gland.
   C   ... pituitary gland.
   [1]

3. True or False? "Some characteristics can be controlled by a single gene."
   A   True
   B   False
   [1]

4. Which one of these things do animals not compete for in order to survive?
   A   Food
   B   Light
   C   Space
   [1]

5. Which of the following is produced by deamination in the liver?
   A   Glucose
   B   Ammonia
   C   Sodium
   [1]

6. True or False? "Quadrats can be used with transects."
   A   True
   B   False
   [1]

7. Which of the following is the main reproductive hormone in men?
   A   Oestrogen
   B   Progesterone
   C   Testosterone
   [1]

8. What is a gene?
   A   An amino acid
   B   A protein
   C   A small section of DNA
   [1]

9. Explain what is meant when a species is described as being 'extinct'.

   ....

   ....
   [1]

10. Alex has an X chromosome and a Y chromosome. Is Alex biologically male or female?

    ....
    [1]

11. What is Type 2 diabetes?

    ....

    ....
    [1]

12. Describe the process of natural selection.

    ....

    ....

    ....

    ....

    ....

    ....
    [4]

Test 29: Paper 2 Mixed Topics

There are **11 questions** in this test. Give yourself **10 minutes** to answer them all.

1. True or False? "Living things remove materials from the environment, and these are recycled back into the environment by microorganisms."

    A True

    B False

    [1]

2. What effect does ADH have on kidney tubules?

    A It causes less water to be reabsorbed from them.

    B It causes ions to be reabsorbed from them.

    C It causes more water to be reabsorbed from them.

    [1]

3. True or False? "We have fossil evidence of every species that ever lived."

    A True

    B False

    [1]

4. Non-coding parts of DNA can...

    A ... code for proteins.

    B ... code for lipids.

    C ... switch genes on and off.

    [1]

5. What are Mendel's 'hereditary units' now known as?

    A Genes

    B Ribosomes

    C Mitochondria

    [1]

6. True or False? "Organisms have adaptations that allow them to survive in their own habitats."

    A True

    B False

    [1]

7. Which type of cell division produces gametes?

    A Meiosis

    B Mitosis

    [1]

8. What is the male gamete in plants called?

    A Egg

    B Stamen

    C Pollen

    [1]

Mixed Tests for Paper 2

9. Give one use of genetically engineered bacteria in medicine.

   ....
   [1]

10. A mutation may result in a change in the shape of a protein.
    Give one type of protein this could affect and describe how its function could be affected.

    ....

    ....
    [2]

11. Rachael and Henry are about to have a child. Both of them carry the cystic fibrosis allele, but do not have the disease.
    Complete the genetic diagram to show the possible genotypes of the child.

    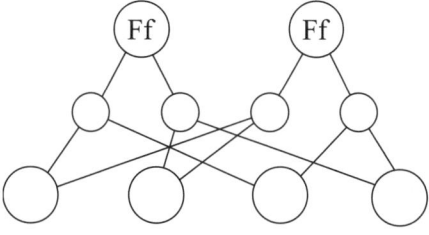

    What is the chance that their child will have cystic fibrosis?
    Explain your answer.

    ....

    ....

    ....
    [4]

Test 30: Paper 2 Mixed Topics

There are **11 questions** in this test. Give yourself **10 minutes** to answer them all.

1. True or False? "The theory of evolution says that all living species have evolved from simple life forms."

   A True

   B False

   [1]

2. Who developed the three-domain classification system?

   A Carl Linnaeus

   B Carl Woese

   C Charles Darwin

   [1]

3. How could a farmer grow crops which are resistant to insect attacks and herbicides?

   A By planting the crops in winter.

   B By putting a large fence around their field.

   C By growing GM crops.

   [1]

4. True or False? "Synapses connect receptors."

   A True

   B False

   [1]

5. What are alleles?

   A Male sex chromosomes

   B Two gametes fused together

   C Different versions of the same gene

   [1]

6. In what type of reproduction do gametes fuse together?

   A Asexual

   B Sexual

   [1]

7. What do receptors in the thermoregulatory centre detect?

   A The temperature of the skin.

   B The temperature of the blood.

   C The temperature of the air.

   [1]

8. Roughly, what percentage of the biomass from a trophic level is transferred to the trophic level above?

   A 0%

   B 10%

   C 50%

   [1]

9. What does an effector do?

   ....
   [1]

10. Suggest two reasons why it is important to understand the human genome.

    1. ....

    ....

    2. ....

    ....
    [2]

11. Describe the process of *in vitro* fertilisation (IVF).

    ....

    ....

    ....

    ....

    ....
    [4]

Answers

Topics for Paper 1
Test 1: Cell Biology
Pages 2-3
1. B *[1 mark]*
2. A *[1 mark]*
3. B *[1 mark]*
4. C *[1 mark]*
5. B *[1 mark]*
6. A *[1 mark]*
7. A *[1 mark]*
8. B *[1 mark]*
9. Any one from: e.g. sterilise the Petri dish/culture medium before use. / Sterilise the inoculating loop before use. / Lightly tape on the lid of the Petri dish. / Store the Petri dish upside down. *[1 mark]*
10. A stem cell is an undifferentiated cell that can divide to produce more undifferentiated cells *[1 mark]* that can differentiate into other types of cell *[1 mark]*.
11.

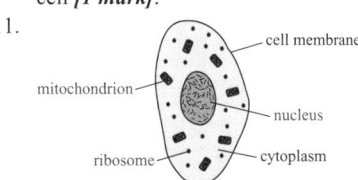

[1 mark for each correct label]
Mitochondria are where most of the reactions for aerobic respiration take place *[1 mark]*. The nucleus contains the genetic material that controls the activities of the cell *[1 mark]*.

Test 2: Cell Biology
Pages 4-5
1. A *[1 mark]*
2. A *[1 mark]*
3. B *[1 mark]*
4. C *[1 mark]*
5. A *[1 mark]*
6. B *[1 mark]*
7. A *[1 mark]*
8. A *[1 mark]*
9. Any one from: e.g. there is a risk of the stem cells being infected with viruses and these being passed on to patients. / Some people feel that human embryos shouldn't be used to create stem cells as each one is a potential human life *[1 mark]*.
10. E.g. a higher resolution means that cells/subcellular structures can be studied in more detail *[1 mark]*.
11. E.g. a nerve cell is long to cover more distance. / A nerve cell has branched connections at its ends to connect to other nerve cells. *[1 mark]*
12. The concentration of mineral ions in the soil is usually lower than inside the root cells *[1 mark]*, so the mineral ions won't diffuse into the cells *[1 mark]*. However, plants need these mineral ions for healthy growth *[1 mark]* so they use active transport to absorb mineral ions against the concentration gradient *[1 mark]*.

Test 3: Organisation
Pages 6–7
1. B *[1 mark]*
2. A *[1 mark]*
3. A *[1 mark]*
4. C *[1 mark]*
5. B *[1 mark]*
6. C *[1 mark]*
7. A *[1 mark]*
8. B *[1 mark]*
9. Protease enzymes catalyse the breakdown of proteins into amino acids *[1 mark]*.
10. Phloem tissue transports (dissolved) sugars from the leaves to the rest of the plant *[1 mark]*.
11. Any two from: e.g. red blood cells / white blood cells / platelets *[2 marks]*
12. Some of the bonds holding the enzyme together break *[1 mark]*. This changes the shape of the enzyme's active site *[1 mark]*. As the enzyme's active site is essential to its function, it won't work anymore *[1 mark]*.

Test 4: Organisation
Pages 8-9
1. B *[1 mark]*
2. B *[1 mark]*
3. B *[1 mark]*
4. C *[1 mark]*
5. C *[1 mark]*
6. B *[1 mark]*
7. B *[1 mark]*
8. A *[1 mark]*
9. E.g. artificial hearts are made from materials such as metal and plastic so they're less likely to be rejected by the body's immune system *[1 mark]*.
10. E.g. drinking too much alcohol *[1 mark]*.
11. A benign tumour is a mass of abnormal cells that doesn't invade other tissues in the body *[1 mark]*.
12. Increasing air movement would increase the rate of transpiration *[1 mark]* because water vapour surrounding the leaf would be swept away *[1 mark]*. This would increase the concentration gradient between water inside and outside the leaf *[1 mark]*, meaning that more water would diffuse out of the leaf *[1 mark]*.

Test 5: Organisation
Pages 10–11
1. A *[1 mark]*
2. A *[1 mark]*
3. C *[1 mark]*
4. B *[1 mark]*
5. C *[1 mark]*
6. C *[1 mark]*
7. C *[1 mark]*
8. A *[1 mark]*
9. In the wall of the right atrium *[1 mark]*.
10. Any two from: e.g. stress / diet / life situation (e.g. lack of money) *[2 marks]*.
11. Any two from: e.g. arteries carry blood away from the heart, whilst veins carry blood to the heart. / Arteries have thick walls, whilst veins have thin walls. / Veins contain valves, but arteries don't. *[2 marks]*
12. Statins reduce the amount of 'bad' cholesterol present in the bloodstream *[1 mark]*. This makes it less likely that fatty deposits will form inside coronary arteries, which is the cause of coronary heart disease *[1 mark]*.

Test 6: Infection and Response
Pages 12–13
1. A *[1 mark]*
2. A *[1 mark]*
3. C *[1 mark]*
4. B *[1 mark]*
5. A *[1 mark]*
6. C *[1 mark]*
7. B *[1 mark]*
8. B *[1 mark]*
9. Measles is spread by droplets from an infected person's sneeze or cough *[1 mark]*.
10. Tobacco mosaic virus causes a mosaic pattern/discolouration on a plant's leaves *[1 mark]*. This affects growth as it means the plant can't photosynthesise as it otherwise could *[1 mark]*.

Answers

11. Mosquitoes are vectors of the protist/pathogen that causes malaria *[1 mark]*. Mosquito nets help to stop people from being bitten by mosquitoes, which stops them from being infected with the protist/pathogen *[1 mark]*.
12. A lack of nitrate causes stunted growth *[1 mark]* because nitrate ions are needed to make proteins, which are essential for growth *[1 mark]*.

Test 7: Infection and Response
Pages 14–15

1. B *[1 mark]* 2. A *[1 mark]*
3. B *[1 mark]* 4. C *[1 mark]*
5. B *[1 mark]* 6. B *[1 mark]*
7. C *[1 mark]* 8. A *[1 mark]*
9. Viruses live inside your cells and replicate themselves *[1 mark]*. The cell then bursts, releasing all the viruses, and this cell damage is what makes you feel ill *[1 mark]*.
10. The nose contains hairs / mucus *[1 mark]*, which trap particles that could contain pathogens *[1 mark]*.
11. The dead or inactive pathogens that the vaccine contains carry antigens *[1 mark]*. White blood cells produce antibodies in response to these antigens *[1 mark]*. If the same type of pathogens appear after that, the white blood cells can quickly mass-produce the same antibodies to kill the pathogens *[1 mark]*.

Test 8: Infection and Response
Pages 16–17

1. A *[1 mark]* 2. B *[1 mark]*
3. C *[1 mark]* 4. C *[1 mark]*
5. A *[1 mark]* 6. B *[1 mark]*
7. A *[1 mark]* 8. C *[1 mark]*
9. By using fungicides / destroying infected leaves *[1 mark]*.
10. A double-blind trial is where neither the doctor nor the patient *[1 mark]* knows whether the patient is getting the drug or the placebo until the results are gathered *[1 mark]*. This is so that the doctors monitoring the patients aren't influenced by their knowledge *[1 mark]*.

11. Monoclonal antibodies can be made that will bind to tumour markers on cancer cells *[1 mark]*. These monoclonal antibodies can have a radioactive substance/toxic drug/chemical attached *[1 mark]*, which will kill the cancer cells/stop the cancer cells from growing and dividing *[1 mark]*.

Test 9: Bioenergetics
Pages 18–19

1. C *[1 mark]* 2. C *[1 mark]*
3. A *[1 mark]* 4. A *[1 mark]*
5. A *[1 mark]* 6. A *[1 mark]*
7. C *[1 mark]* 8. A *[1 mark]*
9. Because the body can't supply enough oxygen to the muscles *[1 mark]*.
10. Cellulose *[1 mark]*. The cell wall is made using this material *[1 mark]*.
11.
$$\text{carbon dioxide} + \text{water} \xrightarrow{\text{light}} \text{glucose} + \text{oxygen}$$

[2 marks for whole equation completed correctly, 1 mark for one or two gaps filled correctly.]
12. Blood flowing through the muscles transports the lactic acid to the liver *[1 mark]*. In the liver, lactic acid is converted to glucose *[1 mark]*.

Test 10: Bioenergetics
Pages 20-21

1. B *[1 mark]* 2. B *[1 mark]*
3. C *[1 mark]* 4. C *[1 mark]*
5. B *[1 mark]* 6. C *[1 mark]*
7. B *[1 mark]* 8. A *[1 mark]*
9. Metabolism is the sum of all of the reactions that happen in a cell or the body *[1 mark]*.
10. It will slow down *[1 mark]* because there will be less light present to transfer the energy needed for photosynthesis *[1 mark]*.
11. Muscle fatigue is where the muscles tire and can no longer contract efficiently *[1 mark]*. It can occur after large periods of exercise *[1 mark]*.

12. Any two from: e.g. in chemical reactions to build up larger molecules from smaller ones. / To allow the muscles to contract/for movement. / To keep body temperature steady in colder surroundings/to keep warm. *[2 marks]*

Mixed Tests for Paper 1
Test 11: Paper 1 Mixed Topics
Pages 22-23

1. C *[1 mark]* 2. C *[1 mark]*
3. B *[1 mark]* 4. A *[1 mark]*
5. B *[1 mark]* 6. A *[1 mark]*
7. C *[1 mark]* 8. B *[1 mark]*
9. Any two from: It may have a thin membrane. / It may have a large surface area. / It may have lots of blood vessels. / It could be ventilated. *[2 marks]*
10. Glucose is combined with nitrate ions from the soil *[1 mark]* to make amino acids, which are made into proteins *[1 mark]*.
11. Malignant tumours are cancerous *[1 mark]*. They invade neighbouring tissues in the body *[1 mark]*, and break off and spread to other parts of the body forming secondary tumours *[1 mark]*.

Test 12: Paper 1 Mixed Topics
Pages 24-25

1. C *[1 mark]* 2. A *[1 mark]*
3. A *[1 mark]* 4. C *[1 mark]*
5. A *[1 mark]* 6. B *[1 mark]*
7. C *[1 mark]* 8. B *[1 mark]*
9. Any one from: e.g. skin / nose / stomach / trachea and bronchi *[1 mark]*.
10. Not enough oxygen is supplied to the muscles *[1 mark]*, so they start respiring anaerobically *[1 mark]*. This means that there's an incomplete breakdown of glucose, which produces lactic acid *[1 mark]*.
11. Layers of fatty material build up inside the coronary arteries, narrowing them *[1 mark]*. This reduces the flow of blood through the coronary arteries *[1 mark]*, resulting in a lack of oxygen for the heart muscle *[1 mark]*.

Answers

Test 13: Paper 1 Mixed Topics
Pages 26-27

1. A *[1 mark]*
2. A *[1 mark]*
3. B *[1 mark]*
4. C *[1 mark]*
5. B *[1 mark]*
6. A *[1 mark]*
7. C *[1 mark]*
8. B *[1 mark]*
9. Cell differentiation is the process by which cells become specialised for a particular function *[1 mark]*.
10. E.g.
    Disease: Salmonella food poisoning / Gonorrhoea *[1 mark]*
    Symptoms:
    For Salmonella food poisoning any one from: e.g. fever / stomach cramps / vomiting / diarrhoea.
    For gonorrhoea: any one from: e.g. pain when urinating / thick yellow or green discharge from the vagina or penis. *[1 mark]*
11. Function: Xylem vessels transport water and mineral ions from the roots to the leaves *[1 mark]*.
    Adaptation: The cells form hollow tubes to allow water and mineral ions to pass through. / The tubes are strengthened by lignin. *[1 mark]*
12. Osmosis is the movement of water molecules across a partially permeable membrane *[1 mark]* from a region of higher water concentration to a region of lower water concentration *[1 mark]*.

Test 14: Paper 1 Mixed Topics
Pages 28-29

1. B *[1 mark]*
2. B *[1 mark]*
3. C *[1 mark]*
4. A *[1 mark]*
5. B *[1 mark]*
6. A *[1 mark]*
7. C *[1 mark]*
8. A *[1 mark]*
9. The valve allows blood to flow in both directions not just forwards *[1 mark]*.
10. It increases the rate of diffusion *[1 mark]*, because more particles can pass across the exchange surface at once *[1 mark]*.
11. Pulmonary vein *[1 mark]*
    Aorta *[1 mark]*
12. A tumour cell *[1 mark]* and a B-lymphocyte *[1 mark]*.

Test 15: Paper 1 Mixed Topics
Pages 30-31

1. C *[1 mark]*
2. B *[1 mark]*
3. B *[1 mark]*
4. A *[1 mark]*
5. B *[1 mark]*
6. A *[1 mark]*
7. A *[1 mark]*
8. C *[1 mark]*
9. $$\text{magnification} = \frac{\text{size of image}}{\text{size of real object}}$$
    [1 mark]
10. Any two from: Cardiovascular disease / lung disease / lung cancer *[2 marks]*
11. E.g. temperature *[1 mark]*.
    By using a water bath / an electric heater. *[1 mark]*
12. 2 hours = 60 × 2 = 120 minutes
    120 ÷ 20 = 6 divisions *[1 mark]*
    $2^6 = 2 \times 2 \times 2 \times 2 \times 2 \times 2$
    = 64 cells *[1 mark]*

Topics for Paper 2
Test 16: Homeostasis and Response
Pages 32-33

1. B *[1 mark]*
2. A *[1 mark]*
3. A *[1 mark]*
4. C *[1 mark]*
5. B *[1 mark]*
6. C *[1 mark]*
7. C *[1 mark]*
8. A *[1 mark]*
9. E.g. water content of the blood. Core body temperature. Blood sugar level. *[1 mark each]*
10. Type 1 diabetes is a condition where the pancreas doesn't produce enough insulin, or doesn't produce any insulin at all *[1 mark]*. This is dangerous because it means that a person's blood sugar level can rise to a level that can kill them *[1 mark]*.
11. Long-sightedness is where people are unable to focus on near objects *[1 mark]* because the images of near objects/rays of light are brought into focus behind the retina *[1 mark]*.

Test 17: Homeostasis and Response
Pages 34-35

1. B *[1 mark]*
2. A *[1 mark]*
3. C *[1 mark]*
4. A *[1 mark]*
5. B *[1 mark]*
6. B *[1 mark]*
7. C *[1 mark]*
8. A *[1 mark]*
9. It stimulates the release of an egg from the ovary *[1 mark]*.
10. Homeostasis is the regulation of conditions inside the body *[1 mark]* to maintain a stable internal environment *[1 mark]* in response to changes in internal and external conditions *[1 mark]*.
11. The blood vessels supplying the skin (capillaries) dilate *[1 mark]* so that more blood flows close to the surface of the skin *[1 mark]*. This transfers energy from the body to the environment, helping to lower body temperature *[1 mark]*.

Test 18: Homeostasis and Response
Pages 36-37

1. A *[1 mark]*
2. B *[1 mark]*
3. B *[1 mark]*
4. A *[1 mark]*
5. C *[1 mark]*
6. A *[1 mark]*
7. B *[1 mark]*
8. C *[1 mark]*
9. E.g. Dialysis treatment, which artificially filters the patient's blood to keep the concentration of dissolved substances at normal levels. / Kidney transplant, where the damaged kidney is exchanged for a healthy kidney from a donor. *[1 mark]*.
10. E.g. Plant B would be growing sideways/bent whereas plant A would be growing straight up *[1 mark]*.
    Explanation: Auxin accumulates on the shaded side in plant B *[1 mark]*. This causes cells on this side to grow/elongate faster, so plant B bends towards the light *[1 mark]*.
11. A motor neurone *[1 mark]*.
    Examples: Muscle (e.g. biceps) / A gland (e.g. adrenal gland) *[1 mark]*. Muscles contract (e.g. biceps contract to bend arm) / Glands secrete hormones (e.g. adrenal gland secretes adrenaline) *[1 mark]*.

Test 19: Inheritance, Variation and Evolution
Pages 38-39

1. B *[1 mark]*
2. C *[1 mark]*
3. C *[1 mark]*
4. A *[1 mark]*
5. A *[1 mark]*
6. A *[1 mark]*
7. C *[1 mark]*
8. B *[1 mark]*

Answers

9. Any two from: It has been shown that characteristics/traits are passed on to offspring in genes. / There is evidence in the fossil record. / Because we know how antibiotic resistance evolves in bacteria. *[2 marks]*
10. Any two from: It creates a prejudice that those with a genetic disorder are 'undesirable'. / It may lead to a culture where people select characteristics they want their baby to have (designer babies). / Screening is expensive. *[2 marks]*
11. Asexual reproduction results in offspring which are clones of the parent *[1 mark]*. Sexual reproduction produces variation in the offspring *[1 mark]*. An asexual species would be less able to respond to an environmental change due to a lack of variation *[1 mark]*.

Test 20: Inheritance, Variation and Evolution
Pages 40-41
1. B *[1 mark]*
2. A *[1 mark]*
3. C *[1 mark]*
4. C *[1 mark]*
5. A *[1 mark]*
6. A *[1 mark]*
7. B *[1 mark]*
8. C *[1 mark]*
9. Fossils are the remains or impressions of plants and animals that were alive thousands of years ago *[1 mark]*.
10. The process in which cells are removed from an embryo and checked to see if the embryo will have certain genetic disorders *[1 mark]*.
11. That characteristics are passed from one generation to the next *[1 mark]* by separately inherited factors which he named 'hereditary units' *[1 mark]*.
12. Each population has a range of alleles that control their characteristics *[1 mark]*. If there are different conditions on either side of the flood, different characteristics will become more common in each population due to natural selection *[1 mark]*. Eventually individuals from each population will become so different that they will no longer be able to interbreed successfully *[1 mark]*.

Test 21: Inheritance, Variation and Evolution
Pages 42-43
1. B *[1 mark]*
2. C *[1 mark]*
3. A *[1 mark]*
4. A *[1 mark]*
5. A *[1 mark]*
6. B *[1 mark]*
7. B *[1 mark]*
8. A *[1 mark]*
9. Any two from: e.g. the environment changes too quickly. / A new predator. / A new disease. / Competition with another, more successful species for resources. / A catastrophic event, e.g. a volcanic eruption. *[2 marks]*
10. They have a common distant ancestor *[1 mark]*. They have different recent ancestors *[1 mark]*.
11. During sexual reproduction two gametes fuse together, producing a new cell *[1 mark]*. This cell contains a mixture of chromosomes — some from the mother, and some from the father *[1 mark]*. This means it inherits a combination of features from each parent, producing variation *[1 mark]*.

Test 22: Inheritance, Variation and Evolution
Pages 44-45
1. C *[1 mark]*
2. B *[1 mark]*
3. C *[1 mark]*
4. A *[1 mark]*
5. C *[1 mark]*
6. B *[1 mark]*
7. A *[1 mark]*
8. B *[1 mark]*
9. A vector is used to insert the gene into the required cells / new organism *[1 mark]*. Example: a bacterial plasmid / a virus *[1 mark]*.
10. The plant will be tall *[1 mark]*, as the tall allele (T) is dominant over the recessive dwarf allele (t) *[1 mark]*.
11. A single nucleotide consists of a sugar *[1 mark]*, a phosphate group *[1 mark]* and one base *[1 mark]*.

Test 23: Ecology
Pages 46-47
1. B *[1 mark]*
2. C *[1 mark]*
3. A *[1 mark]*
4. A *[1 mark]*
5. C *[1 mark]*
6. A *[1 mark]*
7. B *[1 mark]*
8. B *[1 mark]*
9. The amount of biomass at each stage of a food chain decreases as you go up the chain *[1 mark]*.
10. It releases carbon dioxide into the air *[1 mark]*.
11. Any two from: Breeding programmes. / Programmes to regenerate rare habitats. / Programmes to reintroduce field margins and hedgerows to farm land. / Programmes to reduce deforestation. / Programmes to reduce carbon dioxide emissions. / Programmes to encourage people to recycle waste. *[2 marks]*
12. Any three from: New pathogens arriving. / New predators arriving. / A reduction in the availability of food sources. / An increase in the number or type of competitors. *[3 marks]*

Test 24: Ecology
Pages 48-49
1. C *[1 mark]*
2. C *[1 mark]*
3. A *[1 mark]*
4. A *[1 mark]*
5. B *[1 mark]*
6. B *[1 mark]*
7. A *[1 mark]*
8. B *[1 mark]*
9. Any two from: e.g. increasing birth rate. / Changing diets in developed countries. / New pests/pathogens that affect farming. / High input costs of farming. / Conflicts affecting availability of food and water. *[2 marks]*
10. To provide land for cattle / rice crops / farming *[1 mark]*. To grow crops for biofuels *[1 mark]*.
11. It is important to ensure species don't disappear *[1 mark]*.
Explanation: Quotas limit the number of fish that can be caught *[1 mark]* which helps to ensure that numbers don't fall too low *[1 mark]*.

Test 25: Ecology
Pages 50-51
1. A *[1 mark]*
2. A *[1 mark]*
3. C *[1 mark]*
4. A *[1 mark]*
5. B *[1 mark]*
6. A *[1 mark]*
7. A *[1 mark]*
8. B *[1 mark]*
9. Interdependence is where each species in a community depends on one another for something *[1 mark]*.

Answers

10. Any two from: e.g a change in temperature. / A change in the availability of water. / A change in the composition of atmospheric gases. *[2 marks]*
11. When bogs are drained, the peat starts to decompose *[1 mark]*, releasing carbon dioxide which contributes to global warming *[1 mark]*.
12. E.g. they improve crop yield/provide more food *[1 mark]*. They increase the nutritional value of food *[1 mark]*.

Mixed Tests for Paper 2

Test 26: Paper 2 Mixed Topics
Pages 52-53

1. B *[1 mark]* 2. A *[1 mark]*
3. C *[1 mark]* 4. B *[1 mark]*
5. A *[1 mark]* 6. A *[1 mark]*
7. A *[1 mark]* 8. B *[1 mark]*
9. So that your cells and the enzymes in them have the right conditions to function properly *[1 mark]*.
10. It is used to produce a very detailed picture of the brain's structures *[1 mark]*.
11. A few plant cells are put into a growth medium with hormones *[1 mark]* and grow into clones of the parent plant *[1 mark]*.
12. Inbreeding is when closely related individuals are bred together *[1 mark]*. It can lead to health problems *[1 mark]* because it increases the chance that an individual will inherit harmful genetic defects *[1 mark]*.

Test 27: Paper 2 Mixed Topics
Pages 54-55

1. B *[1 mark]* 2. B *[1 mark]*
3. C *[1 mark]* 4. A *[1 mark]*
5. B *[1 mark]* 6. C *[1 mark]*
7. C *[1 mark]* 8. C *[1 mark]*
9. Methane gas *[1 mark]*.

10.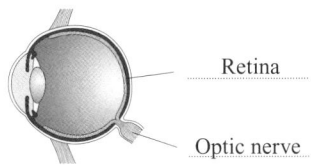
[2 marks]
11. Any two from: e.g. oral contraceptive pill / skin patch / implant / injection *[2 marks]*.
12. Because people aren't immune to the new strain *[1 mark]* and there is no effective treatment *[1 mark]*.

Test 28: Paper 2 Mixed Topics
Pages 56-57

1. B *[1 mark]* 2. A *[1 mark]*
3. A *[1 mark]* 4. B *[1 mark]*
5. B *[1 mark]* 6. A *[1 mark]*
7. C *[1 mark]* 8. C *[1 mark]*
9. It's when no individuals of a species remain *[1 mark]*.
10. Alex is biologically male *[1 mark]*. (Females have two X chromosomes, males have an X and a Y chromosome.)
11. Where a person becomes resistant to their own insulin *[1 mark]*.
12. There is genetic variation within a population *[1 mark]* and those individuals with characteristics that make them better adapted to the environment have a better chance of survival *[1 mark]*. They are therefore more likely to survive long enough to breed *[1 mark]* and pass on the genes responsible for the useful characteristic *[1 mark]*.

Test 29: Paper 2 Mixed Topics
Pages 58-59

1. A *[1 mark]* 2. C *[1 mark]*
3. B *[1 mark]* 4. C *[1 mark]*
5. A *[1 mark]* 6. A *[1 mark]*
7. A *[1 mark]* 8. C *[1 mark]*
9. To produce insulin *[1 mark]*.
10. An enzyme *[1 mark]* may no longer be able to bind its substrate *[1 mark]*. / A structural protein *[1 mark]* may lose its strength *[1 mark]*.

11.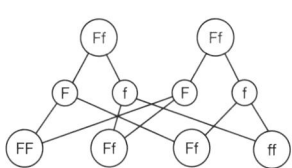
[1 mark for the gametes' alleles being correct and 1 mark for the offspring's genotypes being correct]
As the cystic fibrosis allele is recessive, for the child to have the disease they will need two recessive alleles *[1 mark]*. The diagram shows that the chance the child will have cystic fibrosis is 25%, or 1 in 4 *[1 mark]*.

Test 30: Paper 2 Mixed Topics
Pages 60-61

1. A *[1 mark]* 2. B *[1 mark]*
3. C *[1 mark]* 4. B *[1 mark]*
5. C *[1 mark]* 6. B *[1 mark]*
7. B *[1 mark]* 8. B *[1 mark]*
9. It produces a response to a nervous impulse *[1 mark]*.
10. Any two from: e.g. it allows scientists to identify genes in the genome that are linked to different types of disease. / Knowing which genes are linked to inherited diseases could help us to understand them better and find effective treatments. / Scientists can look at genomes to trace the migrations of certain populations around the world. *[2 marks]*
11. LH and FSH are given to a woman to stimulate several eggs to mature *[1 mark]*. The eggs are collected from the woman's ovaries and fertilised in a laboratory *[1 mark]*. The fertilised eggs are grown into embryos *[1 mark]*. Once the embryos are balls of cells, they are transferred into the woman's uterus *[1 mark]*.